THE BOSS'
GUIDE TO
SMARTER IT

From CEOs to SMBs - The Ultimate Guide to Effortlessly Keeping your technology working and Finding a Professional, Honest, Considerate, Fairly Priced and Dependable Computer Consultant

Printed in the United States of America

First Printing, 2011

ISBN 10: 1468086014
ISBN 13: 9781468086010
Swift Chip, Inc.

433 N. Camden Dr., 6th Fl.

Beverly Hills, CA 90210

www.kenmay.net

Read this guide and you'll discover:

- The five types of technical support available, and the pros and cons of each.

- How to avoid getting ripped off, disappointed, and paying for sub-standard work.

- 12 Warning signs that you hired the wrong computer consultancy.

- Viruses, worms, spyware, and hackers: what you need to know to protect your company from invasion.

- Everything you need to know about IT contracts, payment schedules, and rate negotiations.

- 10 Critical characteristics to look for in a competent computer consultant.

- Why you need to avoid "cheap" or "bargain" computer repair shops.

- How to turn technology into a competitive advantage instead of a drain on your time, money, and resources.

- What are "managed services" and why your business desperately needs it.

Table of Contents

Introduction:

Business Is Becoming More Technical and Complex

There is a powerful force driving all businesses to deliver superior products and services, faster, and on tighter margins - technology.

Every business, from small Mom and Pop stores to large enterprises are developing a growing dependence on technology; whether it's e-mail, e-commerce and websites, database management, or accounting software, there is hardly a business alive today that doesn't have some level of dependence on their computer network and the various applications, services, and data it stores.

The upside of technological advances is tremendous. When applied correctly, technology can provide your business significant competitive advantages in faster production, increased productivity, improved customer service, and up-to-the-minute reporting for strategic planning and decision making.

The Potential Downsides of Technology

The downside of this vast dependence on technology is that when it doesn't work, it can become a tremendous source of frustration, putting a major strain on production, sales, and fulfillment. No business is immune from computer problems and failures. Without proper network maintenance, the average business can end up with spyware, viruses, and system crashes that can easily turn into major network outages lasting for hours; and that's not including the daily computer "glitches" and problems that frustrate you and your employees.

Then, there's the complexity of it all! Installing and supporting even a small, 5-person network requires specialized knowledge and skills that most small business owners don't have in-house, and the margin for error is greatly reduced in a small business. If a large corporation makes a $50,000 technology mistake, it's certainly not a good thing, but it only represents a minor blip in their overall IT budget. If a small business makes a $20,000 or even a $10,000 technology mistake, it significantly impacts their profitability and cash flow!

If you are like most business owners, you probably shy away from most things technical in nature because you don't understand how it works, why it works, and how to operate it. After all, what you want are business solutions to drive sales and profitability; not whiz-bang gadgets and budget-busting non-solutions that break and make your life more complicated. Yet, the technology that runs your business is too important and too expensive to ignore.

- So how do you make sure that the hardware, software and solutions you are investing in actually support your business goals and work the way they are supposed to?

- How do you stay on top of technological advances that will give you significant competitive advantages while steering clear of the "latest and greatest" fads?

- How do you make sure your data is protected from an ever-growing list of threats including viruses, hackers, spyware, faulty

hardware and software, and even employee sabotage?

- And ultimately, how do you go about finding a reliable consultant or consultancy that not only has the technical expertise to make all of this technology work for you, but also the business acumen to recommend and implement real solutions that enhance productivity and profitability?

That is what this book is about. It's about arming you with the basic information you need to find a trusted advisor who can help your small business tame technology and turn it into a powerful, competitive weapon instead of a huge financial strain and source of problems.

The "IT Guy" Horror Stories

Unfortunately, there is no shortage of horror stories about unbelievably bad customer service from technology companies and computer consultants. They range from annoying computer support consultants who take forever to return a phone call to horror stories about fly-by-night computer repair shops or consultants who accidentally delete all of the data stored on a network as a result of their unethical or incompetent behavior. I'm sure if you talk to your own friends and colleagues you will get an ear-full of the unfortunate experiences they have encountered in this area.

The biggest reason for this is that the computer services industry is not regulated like many other industries. Almost anyone who can turn on a computer can set up a computer repair shop regardless of their actual knowledge and expertise. Compare this to automotive repair shops, electricians, plumbers, lawyers, realtors, dentists, doctors, and accountants (to name a few) who are heavily regulated to protect the consumer from receiving substandard work or getting ripped off. However, the computer industry is still very new and there aren't many laws in existence to fully protect the consumer.

The upside is that most computer consultants are ethical and will not try to rip you off or take advantage of you. But unethical computer consultants aren't the biggest problem; *well-meaning, incompetent consultants are.* Even if they are honestly trying to do a good job for you, their inexperience can cost you dearly in inflated support bills, network performance, security, and data loss.

That is where this book will come in handy. It will give you basic, need-to-know facts to help you find an honest, competent consultant who can contribute to your business's success. By arming more business owners with the information contained in this book, I am hoping to raise the standards within the computer repair and support industry, and to give you, the consumer, useful information to help you guard against the unethical or conduct or incompetence of some companies and consultants.

Note: While there are plenty of women in the computer consulting and IT business industries, the large majority are men. For simplicity, we will therefore refer to computer consultants in the masculine gender throughout this book.

You will also notice that we sometimes use the term "computer consultant", and other times we will use the word "technician." Both refer to the guy or gal providing advice, products, services, and support for your computer network. However, "consultant" will be used to define a person or company with a higher level of expertise and knowledge, whereas a "technician" will define someone who simply knows how to fix computers.

What You Will Learn From This Book:

- How to become an educated buyer of IT support and services.

- How to avoid getting ripped off by an incompetent, unethical computer consultant.

- How to reduce your IT costs.

- How to secure your network and data from viruses, spyware, hackers, data loss, natural disasters, and disgruntled employees.

- How to eliminate computer problems and headaches that frustrate you and waste your time.

- How to turn technology into a competitive advantage instead of a drain on your time, money, and resources.

Chapter 1:

The True Cost of Bad Advice, Faulty Repairs, and an Incompetent Computer Consultant

Every business, large or small, depends on technology at some level to operate. If you've owned a computer for more than five minutes, you know that no one is exempt from computer problems, system crashes, and downtime. While all business owners can relate to the sheer frustration these issues create, very few can actually put a dollar figure to the actual hard cost to their business. That is because so much of it is soft costs related to productivity, hours worked, and time lost.

What makes the cost of computer downtime even more difficult to determine is the fact that no business is "average," and therefore statistics that quantify the cost of downtime for the average company are worthless.

However, no business owner can deny the fact that an interruption in their business costs them money, whether that interruption is caused by a server crash, hardware failure, or some other outside force. If you've ever had your business grind to a screeching halt because you and your employees could not access the data or systems necessary for its operations, you must have some idea of the frustration and financial loss to your business even if you didn't put a pencil to figuring out the exact cost.

Take a look at these statistics for a moment:

- Companies experience an average of 501 hours of network downtime every year, and the overall downtime costs an average of 3.6% of annual revenue. *(Source: The*
- *Costs of Enterprise Downtime, Infonetics Research)*

- 93% of companies that lost their data center for 10 days or more due to a disaster filed for bankruptcy within one year of the disaster, and 50% filed for bankruptcy immediately. *(Source: National Archives & Records Administration in Washington.)*

- 20% of small to medium businesses will suffer a major disaster causing loss of critical data every 5 years. *(Source: Richmond House Group)*

- In 2009, 40% of small to medium businesses that manage their own network and use the Internet for more than e-mail will have their network accessed by a hacker, and more than 50% won't even know they were attacked. *(Source: Gartner Group)*

- Of those companies participating in the Contingency Planning & Management Cost of Downtime Survey: 46% said each hour of downtime would cost their companies up to $50,000, 28% said each hour would cost between $51,000 and $250,000, 18% said each hour would cost between $251,000 and $1 million, and 8% said it would cost their companies more than $1million per hour. *(Source: Cost of Downtime Survey Results, 2011.)*

- Cyber-criminals stole an average of $900 from each of 3 million Americans in the past year, and that doesn't include the hundreds of thousands of PCs rendered useless by spyware. *(Source: Gartner Group)*

But even if you don't factor in the soft costs of lost productivity, there is a hard cost of repairing and restoring your network. Most major network repairs will require a minimum of four to eight hours on average to get the network back up and running. Plus, most consultants cannot get on-site to resolve the problem for 24 to 48 hours. That means your network could be down for one to two days.

Since the average computer consultant charges over $130 per hour plus a trip fee and a surcharge if it's an emergency, the average cost of these repairs is $600 to $1,200; and that doesn't even include any software or hardware costs that may also be required. Over a year, this results in $1,800 to $3,600 in costs without even considering hardware and software costs, or other soft costs of lost sales and work hours. Of course, those numbers quickly multiply with larger, more complex networks.

The Cost of Bad Advice

In addition to downtime, there is another cost that most business owners don't consider: the cost of bad advice. That is whenever an inexperienced consultant recommends a product, service, or project that is unnecessary or incorrect for your specific situation.

Another form of bad advice is when a computer consultant doesn't take into consideration all of the pitfalls and situations that will arise when implementing your project, and grossly underestimates the time and money it will take to successfully complete it. When a consultant makes this mistake, your project ends up way over schedule, and costs you two to three times as much in unexpected fees, hardware, and software.

It's gotten so bad that the publication *Network World* recently noted that "increasingly, IT customers are crying malpractice and railing against slipped implementation schedules, compounded consulting fees, and disappointing product performance."

Paying for bad advice is a cost that is also hard to measure. However, if you've ever been disappointed or outright burned by a so-called IT expert, you know the costs to your business are painfully high.

Here are just a few of the ways bad IT advice can cost you:

- Paying for unnecessary projects, software, or hardware.

- Paying too much for repairs, software, and hardware.

- Too much downtime, unstable networks, data loss, and security breaches.

- Getting stuck with a "solution" that doesn't really solve your problems.

- Increasing the time and effort you and your employees invest in rolling out a project.

- Paying double to have a competent consultant fix what the first guy messed up, or complete the project you originally wanted implemented.

- Litigation costs of getting your money back from a consultant who ripped you off.

- The sheer frustration of dealing with the problems resulting from poor advice.

- Dealing with the Sheer frustration of the problems resulting from poor advice.

In some cases, you can put a hard dollar amount to these situations, such as having to hire another consultant to clean up the mess from the first guy. Unfortunately, the other costs are harder to determine.

The trouble is, it's hard to know that you're paying for bad advice until you are already neck deep into the problems. By the time you get the first inkling that you've hired the wrong guy, you've already invested a considerable amount of time and money, making it difficult if not impossible to can the project and look for someone else. That is why the information in this book is so critical: your best defense against all of this heartache is to become an educated consumer that does his homework.

Chapter 2:

What Are Your Options for Technical Support?

With the constant changes to technology and the daily development of new threats, even a small network requires ongoing maintenance from a highly-trained technician to ward off viruses, spam, spyware, slowness, user errors, and data loss. Of course, obviously the costs of hiring a full-time IT person are not always feasible for small to medium businesses. If your business cannot justify hiring a full-time IT manager, you only have three main options for computer support:

Option #1: Don't do anything.

This is really foolish but we see it every day. There are businesses that don't pay any attention to the care and maintenance of their network until it stops working. Then they are forced to call in an expert to repair or replace whatever caused the problem.

This reactive model of network support is similar to ignoring oil and filter changes in your car until smoke starts pouring out from under the hood. Taking a reactive approach to network maintenance is a surefire path to extensive downtime, lost data, and excessive spending on IT support, not to mention major disruptions in staff productivity, sales, production, and customer service.

Even if your computer network appears to be working fine, there are a number of daily, weekly, and monthly maintenance tasks that must to be performed to keep your data secure and your system running smoothly. A short list of these tasks includes:

- Virus scans and updates
- Security patches and updates
- System backups and disaster recovery planning
- Backup verification and maintenance
- Spyware detection and removal
- Server and desktop optimization
- Employee policies and monitoring
- Intrusion detection
- Spam filtering

If you run specialized practice management, CRM (customer relations management), production software, or if you have multiple locations, a wireless network, highly sensitive data (like financial or medical organizations) or other specialized needs, the list will get longer. Remember, your computer network is just like your car or your house. They all need regular maintenance to avoid problems.

If there is any one lesson you learn from this book, I hope it will be to *proactively* monitor, maintain, and secure your network instead of choosing to react to network and computer problems as they arise. Aside from a telephone, the computer network in your office and the data on it are undoubtedly the most important business tools in your office. When they are unavailable, all productive work comes to a grinding halt.

As the old saying goes, 'an ounce of prevention is worth a pound of cure' and this goes double for your computer network. Unfortunately, most business owners are under the incorrect assumption that regular computer maintenance is not necessary and therefore only call in an experienced consultant when something breaks or stops working properly. As we stated previously, this model of "break-fix" computer support is not a good idea, especially if the operation of your network and the data on it are important to your business.

Option #2: Do it yourself.

Although this option is better than doing nothing, it still puts you at risk for computer network disasters. Instead of hiring a qualified consultant to support your network, you designate the most technically-savvy person on staff to be your make-shift IT manager, and only bring in outside help when you run into a network crisis you can't solve.

The problem is, you are pulling this person away from the real job you hired them to do, and unless they have the time to stay up-to-date on the latest developments in IT support, security, and management, they don't have the skills or time required to properly maintain and secure your network and *could actually make things worse*. This inevitably results in a network that is ill-maintained and unstable, which then results in excessive downtime, overspending on IT support, and expensive recovery costs.

Another variation of this is to get your neighbor's kid or a friend to provide computer support on a part-time basis. This is a mistake for two reasons. First, they may not be fully qualified to handle the job and could possibly make things worse. They may be able to fix the problem in the short term, but they might not have the time or expertise to get to the root of the problem. Second, they may not always be available when you need them. If your server goes down at 9:00am, they might not be able to help you until later on that day or evening, causing you to lose a full day's productivity.

Also, as mentioned previously, they are providing reactive support. As with all things in life and business, it is far less expensive to prevent problems than to clean them up after they've happened. If your part-time technician is not performing regular maintenance and monitoring of your network, you are still very susceptible to more problems.

Option #3: Outsource your support to a competent consultant.

Obviously this is going to be the fastest and surest way to solve your computer problems. However, there are an ever-growing number of companies springing up across the country offering computer repair services and support which makes it difficult for a business owner to know which vendor is right for them.

As it stands today, there are **5 different types** of computer support vendors that you can use. In the next section, I'm going to outline what they are, and the pros and cons of each.

Vendor Support:
This would be phone support provided by Dell, Gateway, Microsoft, or any of the big software and hardware vendors. If you've ever tried to get technical support from a large manufacturer or store, you know how frustrating it can be.

First, many vendors do not provide free support. If they do, it usually is very limited and only available by e-mail or web response forms. If you are lucky enough to get phone support, you'll end up going through a maze of phone options before you get a live person, and then the person is usually a non-technical customer service representative who can't provide any real assistance or support. In most cases, they'll be located in India or some other country, and may even be difficult to understand.

Many technology companies outsource their customer service to companies in India because it is much cheaper than employing US workers. You'll also get a different person every time you call, and most will not have any particular knowledge about your business or what you are trying to achieve.

Here's another problem with vendor support: they aren't going to help you solve problems that aren't related directly to their hardware or software. For example, let's suppose you have a problem connecting to the Internet so you call your local Internet provider. If their service is not causing the problem, you're stuck. Maybe your firewall is not configured properly. Maybe the cable is not connected properly. If your problem is even partially related to another software or piece of hardware on your system, they can't and won't help you. The concept of 'Holistic technology care' is entirely missing here.

Computer Support Hotline Services:
These services work like pre-paid calling cards.
For a set fee, you'll get an 800 number to call for 24-7 technical support.
Sounds reasonable, but it's not all it's cracked up to be.

If you are a home user with simple application problems and questions, this service may work well for you. However, if you are a business with mission-critical data, the last thing you want is a junior technician giving you advice. Also, some problems simply need to be analyzed on-site. Finally, these services are set up to deliver basic computer support; not to troubleshoot server problems, help with data recovery, or provide proactive maintenance.

The Part-Time Guy or Technician Just Getting Started:

This is usually a guy who left his job in the IT department of a company, got fired, or lost his job due to a company downsizing. Either way, this person decided to start his own business with the dream of making lots of money providing computer support to small businesses.

In many cases, these guys will try to do a good job for you. They are well meaning and will often work cheap. They are usually eager to please and will do their best to make you happy. They might even have been referred to you by a friend or business colleague.

Although they have every intention of providing you with a good service, there are some things you need to consider before hiring them to work on your network. Since most of these guys work from home, they don't have a secretary or office staff to handle your requests. When you call, you will either get:

- An answering machine.

- A wife, girlfriend, or child who will take a message (with you not knowing if it will ever reach him).

- No answer and no voice mail; the phone just keeps ringing.

- The consultant on his cell phone. Unfortunately, he's usually at another client's site, in his car, or taking care of some personal business (you catch him at his doctor's office or in a noisy restaurant).

The problem with this is response time. If you have a major network crisis, you need to know that you can get in touch with your consultant AND get a call back or response immediately. But it doesn't end there…

Another problem you'll encounter is availability; he might not always be around when you need him. What happens if he goes on vacation or gets sick? What happens if two or more of his clients experience a major emergency at the same time? Or, what happens if the going gets tough and he decides to take another job? These are all scenarios that happen frequently with computer consultants who haven't truly established best-practices and systems in their businesses; and if they are only supporting your network part-time, you can bet your emergency is going to take a back seat to their full-time employer.

Guaranteeing their work is another problem. Most of these guys do not have a professional contract, proposal, or invoice to give you, which means you have no written paperwork or contractual agreements to fall back on if things go wrong. Plus, most do not carry insurance, and cannot compensate you if they accidentally screw up your network or cause you to lose data. Without workers compensation or liability insurance, you become completely liable if they get hurt working in your office. That means they can actually take you to court and sue you for damages!

Even if they guarantee their work, how do you know they'll be around to fulfill their promises? Addresses and phone numbers can be changed instantly, and your one-man- wonder can disappear leaving you no recourse or recovery.

The Big "Major Player" Tech Support Company:
This vendor is the complete opposite of the one-man-band. They may have multiple technicians, multiple locations, and a support crew.

They might even have locations across the globe. There are many first-rate computer support companies that fall into this category that can be trusted to do a good job for you. As a matter of fact, many have the staff and resources to do an outstanding job.

So what's the problem? Their schedule, price, and availability!

In many cases, these companies are so busy servicing a number of large, profitable clients that they might not give you, the small business owner, the service, response time, and support you want. They also may charge you exorbitant fees to cover their massive overhead of staff and offices. If you are a big business with a big IT budget, you'll do just fine with this type of company. However, if you are a small or medium business with a conservative IT budget, this may not be the best option for you.

Since you don't represent a large windfall of profits for them, they will delegate their junior technicians who are just learning the ropes to support your network, saving the more experienced consultants for their more profitable clients. As a business owner yourself, you can hardly blame them for taking this approach; but as a customer, you don't want to be the small customer who is easily dispensed with.

Just like the big vendors, the larger they get, the less personalized the service becomes. You may not always get the same consultant working on your network, and you might not be able to talk directly with a consultant when you call. Being part of a large franchise doesn't guarantee great service either - it just means they were able to write a check to cover the franchise costs. That doesn't automatically buy them good business sense, technical skills, and customer-focused service.

The Independent Computer Consulting Firm:
You might accuse me of being biased here, but please give me a minute to explain my position before you dismiss my advice.

First of all, I've been doing business in this industry for years and have considerable experience in working with and talking to hundreds of other small business computer consultants. I've seen the horror stories and heard the complaints business owners have with all technology service vendors. Based on that experience, I think the best option for a small-to-midsized business (and in some cases, larger corporations) is an independently owned computer consulting firm that is locally owned and operated.

The business you choose to support your network should be large enough to provide back-up support and fast response times, but small enough to still provide personal service. That is the way we (Swift Chip) modeled our company and have been able to deliver consistent, professional services.

We certainly don't feel as though our model is the only option you can choose, and the size of a company is certainly not the only way to know in advance how professional and competent they will be. There are definitely firms in all of the choices outlined that will do a great job for you. The remainder of this book will further outline what to look for when choosing a computer consultant for your business.

Chapter 3:

Secrets to Choosing a Great Computer Consultant - What to Look For, What to Avoid, and What to Demand!

The most common problem business owners have in finding a competent computer consultant they can trust is lack of knowledge on their side. The majority of business owners are not up-to-date on the latest and greatest technology and how it works, and therefore are ripe for the picking for dishonest or incompetent technicians. They have no way of determining whether or not the consultant they hired is giving them the best possible advice and service. Just like the automotive repair business, computer consultants can easily take advantage of their customers' lack of knowledge by providing substandard services and making poor recommendations.

However, the biggest concern you should have as a business owner is not being ripped off by a con-artist; the person you most need to look out for is a **well-meaning but incompetent consultant.** This type of consultant is not always easy to spot, especially if you are not technically savvy yourself. But with the knowledge outlined in this book and a little bit of research, you will easily be able to weed through all of the consultants vying for your business and choose the one who is going to provide you with the best advice and service.

Why It is Vital to Hire the Right Consultant

We live in a rushed, no-time-to-stop-and-think world of business. Deadlines get shorter while customer expectations expand. Businesses have to produce more with fewer resources in order to compete. Competition is coming at us from every direction, and fickle customers will take their business somewhere else over the simplest oversight or delay.

In this kind of environment, every second counts. You cannot afford to have computer problems or server crashes slowing you down. All business owners depend on their email, databases, accounting software, and other office applications to be fully operational every day. When these applications or processes don't function properly, it can be incredibly frustrating and stressful. It can make you feel completely powerless and at the mercy of your consultant.

When you are in this state of utter helplessness, you are very likely to make a rushed decision and ending up the victim of a dishonest or incompetent consultant. The best time to find a reliable computer consultant is NOT when you are in a dire situation with your back up against the wall.

Plus, the wrong consultant can make things worse. Remember, they are tinkering around with your business's critical and confidential data, documents, and files. You certainly don't want them making a mistake that could cost you far more than a little bit of downtime.

That's why it's so important for you as a business owner to invest a little bit of time to find and choose the right consultant for your business. This little investment of your time will eliminate a lot of hassles, frustration, and money-draining events in the future.

3 Reasons Why Small Business Owners Wind Up Paying for Poor Computer Support

If you are like most business owners, you've paid for computer support services that you were less than satisfied with. Maybe the person you hired didn't really know what they were doing. Maybe they were difficult to contact and let requests slip through the cracks. Maybe they didn't follow up or constantly seemed rushed with you because they were too busy. Maybe it was all of the above.

With the proliferation of computer consultants available, you would think that it would be easy to find someone who is honest, competent, and reliable. Unfortunately, the opposite is true and most business owners settle for mediocre computer consulting services for several reasons.

Reason #1: You know even less about how to find a competent computer consultant than you do about how to fix your own computer problems.
Fortunately, you've invested time and money into this book (or I gave it to you), which will clarify exactly what you need to look for and avoid when choosing a computer consultant. Most business owners do not have this information and therefore make quick, uninformed decisions about who they hire to work on their network and end up paying far more in headaches and bad service.

Reason #2: You believe your business is "too small" to need professional maintenance and support.
The reality is that small businesses are every bit as reliant on the technology that runs their business as large organizations. In most cases, you deal with the same technology-related issues but on a smaller scale. If you can't send and receive e-mail, if you get a virus, if

you lose files, or if you experience a major system melt-down, your business comes to a grinding halt. Communication is halted or greatly hindered. Billable time is lost. Client projects get delayed and deadlines are missed.

Small or large, these types of issues can dramatically add to your stress levels and hurt your bottom line.

Reason #3: You believe you don't have the time to look for another computer consultant.

This is similar to saying you are too busy chopping wood to sharpen the axe.

Here's the truth: it WILL take you more time to fully research and investigate your options and the computer consultants in your area. However, once you've done the work, you'll have a great consultant who will make your life infinitely easier over the long haul.

Use your local Chamber of Commerce, Yelp, Google reviews and LinkedIn to see what others are saying about them. Of course, online reviews can be faked, so having multiple sources of information are always wise.

If you keep hiring second-rate computer consultants, you'll end up having to go through this process time and time again, taking MORE time and costing you more in lost productivity, money, and headaches that it would if you did this process correctly the first time. A great computer consultant is worth their weight in gold, just like a great tax advisor, CPA, or attorney. Surrounding yourself with qualified consultants you can trust is one of the smartest time investments any business owner can make.

10 Critical Characteristics You Should Demand From Your
Computer Consultant: Don't Let Them Touch Your Network Until
You've Confirmed These!

Now that you understand the importance of investing time
into finding the right consultant, let me outline exactly what you need
to look for. There are certain fundamental characteristics about your
consultant that you should absolutely demand, such as insurance,
qualifications, and references. These are very black and white and can
be determined or proven easily.

Then there are other qualifications that are just as important, but are
more of a "gut feeling" determination you will have to make, such as
how well do they communicate with you. In this section, I'm going to
outline all of the characteristics you should demand in order to get the
best possible service and value for your money.

Characteristic #1: Demand Qualifications and Experience

As mentioned earlier, much of the trouble you'll run into with
computer consultants is well-meaning incompetence. There are a lot
of people claiming to be professional computer consultants that
shouldn't be working on business networks. They don't have the right
experience, they've only been doing this type of work for a short period
of time, they don't have the right tools or training, or they don't know
how to fix your specific problem. Whatever their shortcomings are, it
won't turn out well for the business owner that hires them.

Obviously the more experienced your consultant is, the better your
chances are of getting the right repair done quickly. Junior technicians

who offer cheaper prices can take two or three times as long to repair your network (costing you more in the final bill), and may not provide the right recommendations or repairs, which means additional problems and service bills down the road.

Not all networks are the same. Every business has a different mix of hardware, software, and configurations, not to mention specific needs and applications for the technology in their office, which creates an infinite number of scenarios and problems.

The more networks a consultant supports, the more experienced he becomes with a variety of different hardware, software, and network environments. Many junior technicians have only seen one or two different types of networks and therefore are extremely limited in their knowledge of what works and doesn't work. They may not be familiar with the various conflicts, settings, and configurations of your specific anti-virus software, firewall, network settings, or custom applications. They take on your project, full of enthusiasm, only to discover they're in over their head - so they start guessing at what the next steps are. Maybe they take 2 or 3 times as long to get it done. Even then, it may not be done right and then you have to call them back to fix something that should have already been resolved. Inevitably your project ends up costing you way more in additional hardware, software, and labor that you didn't originally anticipate.

How to Determine Your Consultant's True Capabilities:

So how do you know if a consultant is qualified? Ask them the following questions:

1. **How long have they been in business?**
   If they have only been in business for 1 or 2 years, be careful. In most cases, it will take them that long to get fully up to speed. Also, many "one-man-show" consultants may close their doors during these early start up years. You might call their office one day only to find the number has been disconnected or that they've taken a full time job.

2. **Have you worked on my type of network or problem before?**
   You don't want to pay them to learn on your network or project. Ask to speak to other clients they've helped who've had similar problems.

3. **May I see your resume, and the resumes of your technicians?**
   It is perfectly ok to request a resume or summary of qualifications for not only the consultant, but also his staff. Review their resumes the same way you would review a potential employee's resume; after all, they will become an extension of your team and they will be working with your other employees.

4. **What vendor qualifications or certifications do you hold?**
   Hiring a vendor-authorized firm is a good idea for three reasons:

- Authorized dealers are required to uphold higher standards in service and support than their non-certified counterparts, and are closely regulated by the vendors. If you have a complaint about the consultant, you can solicit help from the actual vendor provided the consultant you hired was authorized by them.

- Authorized software dealers are tested on their knowledge by the vendors to ensure a level of competence in installing and supporting their software.

- Authorized dealers have more in-depth knowledge about the products they support because they work with it more frequently than the average consultant. Just keep in mind that a vendor's seal of approval isn't a surefire sign that your consultant is qualified and competent. In addition to vendor certification, you also want to make sure you ask for references.

However, certifications should not be confused with good, old-fashioned experience.

There are plenty of excellent computer consultants who are incredibly talented who don't hold vendor certifications, and there are even more technicians who have plenty of book knowledge but no experience to match. Remember, the skills it takes to pass an exam are a different set of skills than properly diagnosing a business or network problem and solving it as quickly and inexpensively as possible. When possible, always give more weight to actual hands-on experience over vendor certifications.

Quick Tip: If the company you hire has multiple technicians, make sure you know exactly which individual(s) will be assigned to your account, and then ask to see their resume or some other document outlining their experience and qualifications. If possible, get assurance in writing that at least one senior level consultant will be overseeing your project.

Characteristic #2: Demand Client References

This seems obvious, but a lot of business owners skip over this step. Ideally, you want to speak to other clients that have businesses similar to yours, or that have similar projects or problems. Some of the questions you want to ask are:

- Did they deliver on their promises?

- Did they stay on schedule and deliver on time or early?

- Were they responsive and easy to get hold of in times of emergency?

- Did they bill accurately?

- Did they nickel and dime you over every little thing?

- Did they stay within the projected budget?

- Would you use them again?

- Why or why not?

You might also ask if there were any problems that arose and how they handled them.

Not every project goes as planned, but it's not the problem so much as how they handled it when it arose. If your consultant seems hesitant to provide you with references, or if they don't provide client testimonials at a minimum, take that as a red flag.

Characteristic #3: Demand Multiple Technicians

This is important for two reasons. If they don't have other technicians to back them up, you could be left hanging in an emergency. While a "one-man-show" consultant will work cheap, you get what you pay for. In most cases they are far too busy running from one client to the next to do more than a quick Band-Aid fix or to give you the attention and response times you want. If they go on vacation, get sick, or simply get too busy, you could be left hanging in an emergency.

The second reason you want to demand a "team" instead of an individual is because no one technician - no matter how good - has infinite knowledge about every type of software, hardware, and situation. If they have a team of professionals working together on your problem, you have a better chance of getting the job done right.

Characteristic #4: Demand Availability and Fast Response Times

Nothing is more frustrating than having to wait on a consultant to show up when you have a problem. Before hiring a consultant or firm, ask them the following questions:

1. **Do you have a system in place for responding to emergencies?** Look for a company that has a better answer than, "Sure - you can always reach me on my cell phone." Ideally they should have more than one person as a back-up and a customer service person who "owns" the problem and makes sure you get help fast.

2. **How fast is your average response time to an emergency?**
Most companies should easily be able to respond within 1 hour
or less by phone, and should be able to be onsite within 4 hours
or less. Ideally, look for a company that offers remote
management and support. Thanks to new remote management
software tools, many computer consultants can access and
troubleshoot your network remotely, providing faster service in
the event of an emergency.

3. **Do you have a response time guarantee?**
If a computer consultant won't guarantee how fast they can
return your calls, be careful. Most consultants should be able to
guarantee a return call within 2 hours or less. A lack of a
guarantee probably means they also lack a system for handling
and responding to client calls and will leave you high and dry
when you need them the most.

Quick Tip: A good indicator of how responsive they will be to you
in a network emergency is in the sales process. Do they return
your calls promptly? Did they keep their promises? Do they
sound rushed and disorganized when you finally get them on the
phone? If they aren't professional and prompt when proposing
their services, chances are they'll be even worse when providing
them.

4. **Will my dedicated consultant have a backup consultant that is
familiar with my account and network?**
Not only should you have a dedicated consultant for your
account, but you should also have a backup consultant assigned
for times when your dedicated person cannot respond (vacation,
sick days, busy with another account, etc.). Find out in advance
who that person is. If they don't have a team of technicians to
back up your main technician or consultant, proceed with

caution.

Characteristic #5: Demand All Promises in Writing

All too often, certain aspects of a project are discussed verbally such as response time to emergencies, project completion timelines, and how problems will be handled should they arise; yet these are the very things that can come back and bite you later on if they aren't put down in writing.

If your prospective consultant feels that some aspect of your project is unachievable, then it is their responsibility to tell you up-front. By getting them to put everything in writing you can hold them accountable for the promises they make and responsible for outcomes not achieved.

5 Things to Get In Writing:

Payment terms: This includes up-front deposits, fee structure, and payments on completion of the project. Most consultants will ask for an up-front down payment, with the balance in payments as various phases of the project are completed.

Compensation for missed deadlines or faulty work: If they miss a deadline, deliver substandard work, or if you experience problems, how will they make it right? Get it in writing.

Deliverables: What do you expect to be able to do when the project is done? How should the work flow? What does it look like? Don't assume anything. If you expect it to happen, get it in writing and be specific.

Work schedule and pace: Make sure you outline a date for completion as well as the phases of delivery.

Guarantees: What do they guarantee, if anything? Get it in writing.

Any professional firm will be more than happy to outline these items in writing prior to starting a project. If they hesitate or make excuses, it is a sign they are not confident in their ability to deliver on their promises, or that they are not organized to do so.

Characteristic #6: Demand Insurance

All qualified consultants should have two kinds of insurance for your protection. First, they should have workers compensation insurance. If one of their technicians gets hurt at your office and is not covered by their employer's workers compensation insurance, they could sue you for the medical bills and loss of wages.

The consulting firm you hire should also have general business liability insurance. This will protect you in case they make a major mistake and destroy critical company files, equipment, or if they cause a problem that interrupts your business in any way. These mistakes can lead to significant financial loss. Since you cannot get blood from a stone, the consultant might end up going bankrupt and closing their doors leaving you unable to collect damages. Make sure they are insured.

Characteristic #7: Demand a Company That Understands Your Business

Technology should represent more than a bunch of computers networked together. It should be viewed as a strategic tool to improve your productivity, your profits, and your relationships with your customers.

Unless your computer consultant understands the nature of your business, they won't be able to recommend solutions that improve workflow and profits. They can be the most brilliant consultant, but if they don't understand the nature of your business, or if they lack planning, communication, or business skills, you won't get the most from your technology investments. That's why it's critical to find a consultant that has substantial experience in your business, or who at least demonstrates an understanding of it.

Here are some questions to ask yourself to determine if your consultant is truly a business partner, or just a "computer mechanic" applying Band-Aid fixes to your network:

- Do they dig to uncover the source of the problem, or do they only look to fix the surface problem?

- Do they ask thoughtful questions to understand your business processes and discuss workflow with your employees?

- Do they explain how their recommendations will improve your bottom line and speed production, or do they just recommend technology that is "cool?"

- Do they offer training?

- Are they proactive in recommending solutions, or do they wait for you to ask?

- Do they explain their recommendations in simple terms that you can understand, or do they talk over your head using acronyms and terms that don't make sense?

- Do they meet with you quarterly to review your strategic business plans and goals?

- Do they provide case studies of how they helped other businesses achieve strategic competitive advantages or increases in sales, profitability, and production?

- Do they follow up on their work to make sure you were satisfied?

Characteristic #8: Demand a Professional

This may seem silly but I've seen it occur over and over again. A business owner hires a consultant sight unseen. When he shows up at your office, he's dressed sloppily, and looks unshaven, or disheveled. You're almost embarrassed that he's there in your office.

At a minimum, the consultant that you hire should have a neat, clean appearance. At our office, we have a dress code that all consultants must adhere to. Remember, if they are in your office, they are a representation of you and your business. This is especially important if you have clients in your place of business.

Characteristic #9: Demand Detailed Reporting and Invoices.

Every invoice you receive should detail what work was done, why it was done, and the service call or project it was tied to. This will avoid out of control or incorrect billing, as well as sticker shock at the end of the month.

Sloppy, late, or incorrect billing is a sign that your consultant is overwhelmed, not paying attention to detail, or simply doesn't have his act together in his own business. Is that the kind of person you want working on your network? Obviously not. Incorrect billing also adds to your frustration because you'll be forced to review every invoice for accuracy.

Characteristic #10: Demand Clear Communication

Aside from slow or poor response times, lack of communication is the single biggest source of frustration for business owners when dealing with a computer consultant. This can come in many forms but the tragic results are the same. In most cases, your expectations are not met, deadlines slip, and you end up paying for incomplete work that you are not satisfied with.

To avoid these headaches, make sure the consultant you hire has excellent communication skills and makes an effort to thoroughly understand your concerns. He should answer your questions and detail everything you've discussed in writing. Here are some ways to know if the consultant you are considering is a poor communicator:

- Does he frequently use technical terms and acronyms you don't understand?

- Does he ask probing questions about how your business operates, how you use your computer network, and your business goals, or does he stick to the basics?

- Does he explain the reasons behind the recommendations he makes?

- Does he offer you alternative solutions to your problems and explain the pros and cons of each, or does he only push one solution?

- Does he detail everything you've discussed in writing?

- Does he clearly explain how he will do the work and how he will approach and complete your project?

- Does he bring up the downside or potential problems with a particular solution, or does he just talk about the upside?

- Does he provide frequent status updates to your project and/or network or do you have to chase him for answers?

- Does he miss deadlines without an explanation or warning?

If you have any reason to believe that the consultant you plan to hire is not a good communicator, do not hire him for your project.

The Superstar Computer Consultant You Want Vs. A SuperSCREWup You Don't

SuperStar	SuperScrewup
Proven qualifications and experience, vendor certified	Just getting started; less than an year in business, no tangible qualifications
Fully insured (liability and workers' compensation)	No insurance
Several client references	No references and no testimonials
Multiple technicians	No backup team; works alone
Guaranteed response times and documented response systems in place	No response system or guarantees, won't commit to anything
Documents all discussions, deliverables, guarantees, and project timelines in writing	Prefers verbal communication; never follows up with written agreements
Detailed reporting	No reports or status updates
Established office	No office, uses a PO Box and a cell phone
Provides all timelines, prices, and service level guarantees in writing	Vague project outlines, time and materials pricing, "window" timelines
Shows up on time	Shows up too early, late or not at all
Correct, detailed invoices	Invoices are vague, never on time
Easy to reach, returns calls promptly	Hard to reach
Professionally dressed	Sloppy, smelly, disheveled appearance
Systematic follow up to ensure your satisfaction	No follow up; never hear from them unless you call with a problem
Quick and professional problem resolution; stands behind all work for complete customer satisfaction	Apathetic towards problem resolution; no policies or procedures documented for resolving problems

12 Warning Signs of Hiring the Wrong Guy

1. He's defensive or argumentative when you ask about project costs, completion dates, or when you question his recommendations.

2. He won't guarantee his work or your satisfaction.

3. He talks down to you, uses "geek speak," and makes you feel stupid when you question his recommendations or work.

4. He's consistently late, rushed, and misses deadlines without an explanation or apology.

5. He leaves your office a mess (leave wires and cables exposed, doesn't move furniture back).

6. He looks sloppy or disheveled.

7. He uses high pressure or scare tactics to get you to buy.

8. He doesn't explain your options for resolving a problem or completing a project. It's basically his way or the highway.

9. He doesn't follow up after completing a project to make sure you were satisfied.

10. He conducts personal business or supports other clients from your office when he's supposed to be working on your project or network.

11. He never takes a proactive approach to supporting your network, and doesn't offer recommendations to help you secure your network, save money, or improve your company's productivity.

12. He doesn't offer a preventative maintenance or network monitoring program to ensure your network is constantly protected from viruses, hackers, data loss, downtime, or other problems.

Chapter 4:

Avoiding Project Nightmares, Disasters, and Expensive Miscommunications

If you've ever been disappointed or frustrated with a computer consultant's service, this chapter will be of great interest to you.

Small technical "glitches" or repairs can be incredibly frustrating because they seem so small and insignificant, yet they greatly interfere with your ability to get things done. In most cases, business owners may be under the assumption that these tiny problems can be solved quickly, which is not always the case.

If you've hired an incompetent consultant before, you know that simple projects can turn into a full day ordeal, and may even drag out for weeks or more. Unbelievably, your small repair can end up requiring multiple follow-up visits and calls because it occurs again and again, even after it has been "fixed." To make matters worse, they'll charge you for those extra visits even if the issue should have been resolved the first time you paid them to fix it!

This doesn't even take into consideration the inconvenience and downright chaos this causes to your business. Unlike automobile and home repairs, computer network problems can completely disrupt your business, taking you offline for hours or even days.

Or, take this scenario...

You hire a consultant to upgrade your network, but they are way over deadline, and you are still experiencing problems. Only now, they aren't returning your calls promptly and they are acting as if YOU are the problem. Then, to add insult to injury, they ask you for more money!

While you're sitting there waiting for your network to come back online or your project to be completed, your stress level is escalating through the roof because you know your project deadlines and clients aren't going to wait, and it further irritates you that they've not kept the promises they so enthusiastically assured you of in the beginning.

Let's face it: you have a business to run and you don't have the time to deal with technical issues or the incompetence of your consultant. Maybe you have a big proposal that needs to be submitted by the end of the day. Maybe you have client orders that are getting colder by the minute and possibly even ruining client relationships the longer they are delayed. And if you are like most business owners, you are already working behind schedule. The computer problems magnify the stress and delays to a whole new level.

If you've ever been through this type of nightmare before, you know that I'm not exaggerating. To prevent this from happening to you, or to avoid it happening again, you have to identify what causes these situations to happen in the first place. That is what this chapter is all about.

Determine Your Priorities

The first step to avoiding problems is to determine what your "satisfaction priorities" are when working with a computer consultant. Do you place a greater importance on response times or price? Is the quality of the work more important, or do you need it done fast? Is it critical that you have regular updates and status reports on your network, or is a quick e-mail now and again sufficient?

This is not to say that you can't have it all. However, if fast response is a priority to you, then you need to clearly communicate that to your computer consultant *before* you hire them. You should also detail what you consider 'fast' to mean.

Do you expect them to return your call within 15 minutes or 2 hours? Do you expect them to be on-site the same day you call, or within the week? Make sure you are both clear before entering into an agreement. Some computer consulting firms may be more expensive, but may offer a higher quality of workmanship and customer service. Is that acceptable to you? Again, you need to determine this before entering into any project or agreement.

Once you've made a list of the qualities and characteristics that are most important to you, share this list with your prospective consultant because it will help them customize their services to suit you.

About Price...

As with everything in life, you get what you pay for. That is not to say that the most expensive computer consultant will be the best, but you should be cautious if your #1 priority is price. As a consumer, you know first-hand that you are always being offered competitive pricing on all services and products. Businesses compete hard for your dollars and it is only natural for you to think of price first when looking for computer repair and consulting services.

However, services are not like products and cannot be compared like tangible goods such as cars or office equipment. With products, you can compare features and benefits in a fair, apple to apples type comparison. With services, there are too many intangible aspects that cannot be compared easily.

If what you really want is cheap computer support, you can practically guarantee that you're going to have problems. The cheap price won't seem so attractive when you've lost every file on your computer, or if the work has to be redone later when it is discovered that it wasn't done right in the first place.

If you rely heavily on your computer network and the information it contains, then it only makes sense to take time and choose the most *competent* consultant possible, not the cheapest. A quality consultant can give you the expert advice and support you need. They can help lower your company's costs while increasing productivity, customer service, and sales. And, they will be there when you need them.

Start Small

Before you hire your computer consultant to install a new network, hire them to do a small repair or network audit. This will give you the opportunity to see if they show up on time, follow through, and whether or not you like working with them. Never jump into a major project until you've been happy with their work on a smaller project.

Demand a Fixed Price

Many computer consultants charge by the hour for projects instead of quoting a fixed rate. This works great for them but is dangerous for you. Unless you have an established, high-trust relationship with your consultant (or a huge, bottomless pit of money), never agree to this type of contract. This gives your consultant a wide-open field to take as long as they like working on your project - and it actually benefits them if they do. Instead, ask them for a fixed fee where they detail exactly what results they will deliver for an agreed upon budget.

Get Everything in Writing

This is probably one of the single most important things you can do to avoid getting taken advantage of by an incompetent or less than ethical consultant: Get *everything* in writing.
This would include:

- A project timeline and completion date

- A written service guarantee
- An exact budget and payment schedule
- Any and all expectations you have for project deliverables
- When and how you will receive project updates
- Your responsibilities as the client
- What happens if you are not satisfied
- What happens if your project runs over the designated completion date

Do Your Research

Previously we discussed what to look for - actually demand - from your computer consultant. Some of those characteristics will need to be researched - do not skip those steps to save time. Ask your prospective consultant to provide the information you are looking for as part of their proposal. If they don't or aren't willing, cross them off the list of potential partners.

Communicate Your Concerns

Finally, if you have any concerns, questions, or reservations, voice them to your prospective consultant before signing the contract, and ask them to address how they will overcome those concerns if you hire them for the project *in the contract in writing*.

Often people are too shy to say what is really on their mind for fear of appearing rude or unreasonable. If you are concerned that your consultant won't return your calls fast enough, let them know. If you are afraid they might not be able to handle the job, be honest and tell them that. You don't have to be harsh or disagreeable, simply let them know that you have a few concerns, and ask them what they can do to assure you that you won't be disappointed.

Chapter 5:

How to Get the Most Out of Your Computer Consultant

Now that we've outlined what to look for in a qualified, competent, and honest consultant, it makes sense to educate you as to how you can get the most out of your relationship with them.

A great computer consultant will free you from worrying about data loss, downtime, or other problems, allowing you to focus on the more important, strategic aspects of running and growing your business. It will also free your staff from trying to be jacks-of-all-trades and wasting time on activities that they are not particularly good at, which also distracts them from doing the job you hired them for. And ultimately, they will recommend products and solutions that will help your business operate more competitively, increase sales, and lower your workload and stress levels.

But that is not to say you are completely off the hook.

There are a number of ways you can undo everything your consultant has done for you and severely jeopardize the security and reliability of your network. Plus, you are ultimately responsible for making sure your consultant understands your business priorities, goals, and operational systems so that he may offer advice and solutions to support you.

Once you understand your role and responsibilities for maximizing your technology investments, and what your consultant is and is not responsible for, you will have a much better working relationship with them and prevent a number of unpleasant surprises and expensive misunderstandings.

Take Responsibility for Your Own Protection

Many business owners automatically blame their computer or their consultant when they experience a problem, get infected with a virus, or realize their computer has been taken over by spyware. In some cases, these problems are due to negligence on the behalf of your computer consultant.

However, most spyware and virus attacks are the result of an end user downloading a questionable file or program, disabling their anti-virus software, or somehow circumventing security settings or acceptable user policies set by your consultant (such as visiting a peer-to-peer file sharing network like KaZaa, Limewire or BitTorrent).

Many other problems are due to hardware or software inadequacies which cannot be controlled or prevented by your consultant. And finally, many business owners do not want to pay for their consultants to perform simple preventative maintenance, update security patches, update their network, or monitor their system's performance. This lack of maintenance is an invitation for problems that cannot be blamed on your computer consultant.

Unless your consultant has *complete* control over your network and has been given the responsibility to monitor and maintain your network 24-7, chances are that your problems were not caused directly by some action they did (or didn't) take. Again, that is not to say that you are completely at fault for all network problems, but you and your employees need to take an active role in keeping your network and data safe from harm.

Keeping Spyware, Malware, and Viruses off Your Network

In almost every case, malware, spyware, and viruses are able to invade a network because of some action taken by a user. Cyber-criminals are *incredibly clever* and have figured out ways to access your computer network through some of the most innocent and common activities you perform daily.

For example, many of the clients we see infected with a load of spyware simply downloaded a screen saver, an "enhanced" web browser, a music file, or some other "cute" program. In doing so they also unknowingly downloaded a number of spyware and malware programs. Within a short period of time they discovered their computer was running incredibly slowly, and they could no longer use it due to the instability and pop-ups. Your consultant can usually clean up the mess caused by these programs, but it is your responsibility to become educated about what you can and cannot download. Below is a short list of programs and web sites you should never download or visit. Your consultant should be able to provide you with a more comprehensive, up-to-date list:

- Screen savers
- "Enhanced" web browsers like Cool Search
- Emoticons
- Games
- Peer-to-peer file sharing software (KaZaa, Limewire, BitTorrent)
- Music files
- "For fun" web surveys (what type of person are you?)
- Banners that challenge you to "punch the monkey", shoot

something, or answer a trivia question to win a prize
- Enter into a sweepstakes or drawing
- Any software that requires you to accept certain conditions; by agreeing to their conditions, usually outlined in small print, you are agreeing to accept 3rd party software. Make sure you read the conditions you are agreeing to.

Unfortunately, installing the above programs are not the only ways a hacker or malware program can access your computer network. If you do not have the most up-to-date security patches and virus definitions installed on your network, hackers can access your computer through a banner ad or through an e-mail attachment.

Sneaky Ways Hackers Invade Your Network

Not too long ago Microsoft released a security bulletin about three newly discovered vulnerabilities that could allow an attacker to gain control of your computer by tricking users into downloading and opening a maliciously crafted picture. At the same time, Microsoft released a Windows update to correct the vulnerabilities, but if you didn't have a process to ensure you're applying critical updates as soon as they become available, you were completely vulnerable to this attack.

Here's another compelling reason to ensure your network stays up-to-date on the latest security patches…

Most hackers do not discover these security loopholes on their own. Instead, they learn about them when Microsoft (or any other software vendor for that matter) announces the vulnerability and issues an update. That is their cue to spring into action and they immediately go to work to analyze the update and craft an exploit (like a virus) that allows them access to any computer or network that has not yet installed the security patch.

In essence, the time between the release of the update and the release of the exploit that targets the underlying vulnerability is getting shorter every day.

When the "nimda" worm was first discovered back in the fall of 2001, Microsoft had already released the patch that protected against that vulnerability *almost a year before* (331 days). So network administrators had plenty of time to apply the update. Of course, many still hadn't done so, and the "nimda" worm caused lots of damage. But in the summer of 2003 there were *only 25 days* between the release of the Microsoft update that would have protected against the "blaster" worm and the detection of the worm itself!

Clearly, *someone* needs to be paying close attention to your systems to ensure that critical updates are applied as soon as possible. That is why we highly recommend small business owners without a full-time IT staff allow their consultant to monitor and maintain their network.

Create and Enforce an Acceptable Users Policy (AUP)

An AUP (acceptable user's policy) is a written document stating exactly what your employees can and cannot do with company Internet access, computers, and e-mail. For example, employees should not be allowed to download programs, screen savers, pictures, music files, or access file sharing networks, unless needed. This will save precious bandwidth and prevent them from downloading files and programs that contain viruses and spyware. An AUP should also educate them on the appropriate use of your company's resources.

If you don't want your employees to download pornographic material and send racist jokes with a company e-mail account, you have to communicate this information to them in an acceptable user's policy and have them acknowledge *in writing* that they have read and understood it.

There are countless stories of companies being sued for sexual harassment because one employee walked by another employee's desk and saw something offensive on their computer screen. Creating an acceptable user's policy not only ensures your employees know what behavior is acceptable, but it will also help in the prevention of spyware and malware. Your consultant can help you draft this document and enforce the policies outlined.

Allow Your Consultant to Maintain Your Network

As we mentioned previously, many business owners do NOT perform regular maintenance on their computer network; they basically use them until they break and then bring in their consultant.

While this arrangement may seem to work out just fine in the short term, it can dramatically increase problems and the costs of keeping your network running. Then there is the threat of experiencing a major network disaster. Unfortunately, most businesses have to experience some type of major catastrophe before they get serious about maintaining their network. Just ask any business owner about the importance of a solid back-up or keeping their security up-to-date after they've gone through the devastation of losing a week or months' worth of work.

Just look at these alarming statistics:

- **According to recent statistics, approximately 20%** of all small and medium- sized businesses **endure a major network disaster every five years.**

- The U.S. National Fire Protection Agency predicts that **43% of companies that experience these disasters will never reopen, and another 29% will close within three years.**

- If the loss involves data, the diagnosis is even worse. According to the U.S. Bureau of Labor, **93% of companies that suffer a significant data loss are out of business within five years.**

- Over **10,724 new viruses were introduced in 2009,** which is a 52% increase from 2008; and that number is multiplying.

- The Internet Storm Center, which tracks security attacks, reports **7.6 million attacks** in the U.S. alone.

If you really want to protect yourself from losing data, viruses, spyware, hackers, downtime, and a host of other problems, the best thing you can do is find a computer consultant that offers 24-7 monitoring and maintenance for your network and then let them do it for you. By allowing your consultant to control, manage, and maintain your network, the chances of experiencing significant downtime, data loss, or other problems is greatly reduced (more on this in the following chapter on managed services).

Be a Great Client to Have

There is a lot of truth in the cliché, "you'll attract more bees with honey than vinegar." This is especially true when working with professional consultants.

Quite often, business owners take an adversarial approach to working with their vendors. Since they are paying the bills, they believe that they have the right to be demanding, difficult, and even hostile. What they don't realize is that vendor relationships can make or break a company and maintaining a good working partnership with your computer consultant is critical to your business success.

The more respect and appreciation you give your consultant, the more they will want to do a good job for you. Keep in mind that you might need them to do you a special favor or pull you out of a big mess somewhere down the road. If you've developed a good working relationship based on mutual trust and appreciation, they will be far more willing to go the extra mile and help you out when you need it most.

Here are 3 ways to make sure you become a "favorite" client that receives special favors and extra attention:

1. Pay all bills on time or early.

2. Express your gratitude for the work they have done. Everyone likes to know that their efforts are appreciated. If your consultant does an exceptional job, let them know.

3. If you have a complaint, don't jump to the conclusion that your consultant was trying to harm you on purpose. Let them know about

your complaint and give them a chance to make it right before you get angry or take action. It may have been a simple mistake or even an oversight on your behalf.

Overall, clear communication is your best tool to ensure a great working relationship with your computer consultant. You want to find someone you can partner with long-term who will take an active role in making your business profitable and successful. That requires mutual respect on both sides.

7 Ways a Good Relationship with a Competent Computer Consultant Benefits Your Company

1. They proactively monitor and maintain your network to prevent problems from happening in the first place.

2. They are familiar with your network and therefore troubleshoot problems faster.

3. They understand your business and recommend ways to save money, increase productivity, reduce mistakes, and service customers that you haven't even considered.

4. They help lay a good foundation for growing your business.

5. Any changes to your network in the form of adding software or hardware (which are frequently the source of a problem) are known.

6. They sort through all of the new technological breakthroughs, threats, and news and only inform you of the things you need to know.

7. They give you peace of mind knowing that the "gremlins at the gate" are being watched and kept off your network.

Windows Vista

Some users may find they have to "upgrade" their house's windows too!

Chapter 6:

Preventing Disasters with Proactive Maintenance

The computers in your office and the network they are a part of are, without a doubt, the single most important tool you use on a daily basis to run your business. They are at the core of your communications, operations, accounting, client care, and marketing. Just try and imagine one task or operation in your business that does not in some way, directly or indirectly, depend on the security and availability of your computer network.

Yet, as important as it is to your business, very few business owners take a proactive approach to ensuring their network of critical business tools, applications, and processes runs smoothly and as efficiently as possible. This is a huge, costly mistake.

With the constant changes to technology and daily development of new threats, even small peer-to-peer computer networks need on-going maintenance and security updates from a highly-trained consultant.

Unfortunately, what we see most business owners doing is ignoring regular maintenance and only calling in a consultant when something breaks or stops working. It's understandable – many see it as not being worth their time. This reactive model of network maintenance is a surefire path to extensive downtime, lost data, and excessive spending on IT support, not to mention major disruptions in staff productivity, sales, cash flow, production, and customer service that can never be recovered.

How Managed Services Can Prevent These Disasters from Happening to Your Business

Thanks to advances in technology, your computer consultant can now provide on-going remote maintenance and support to maximize the performance, reliability, and stability of your network. The industry term for this is called "managed services," although your consultant might have a different name for it.

The basic premise is this: for a fixed monthly fee, your computer consultant will take over the responsibility of performing regular scheduled maintenance on your network to ensure your virus protection is up-to-date, your back-ups are working properly, that critical security patches are up-to-date, that your firewall and other security settings are actively protecting you, and that all of the components of your network are functioning properly.

They should also be performing regularly scheduled maintenance to maximize the speed and performance of your network, as well as monitoring your network 24 hours a day, 365 days a year to detect, diagnose, and prevent lurking problems from turning into major interruptions to your business.

In essence, they are taking over the tactical, day-to-day maintenance and support of your network for a fraction of the cost of hiring a full-time consultant.

What Are The Benefits of Managed Services?

Service calls to computer networks not under a managed service plan require two to three times as long to diagnose and repair as compared to systems that are under a managed service plan, because of the time required for diagnostics and testing. This naturally leads to higher repair bills and more downtime.

In addition to the added expense and time required to perform these repairs, some of the damage to your network can be irreversible, and could have been easily prevented if a solid managed service plan was in place.

If the data and operation of your network is important to your business, then you need to make sure you are taking the necessary steps to ensure its safety and security; that is what managed services can do for you. A good managed service plan will provide the following benefits:

- **You'll practically eliminate expensive repairs and data recovery costs.** By detecting and preventing network disasters before they happen, a good managed service plan will save you thousands of dollars in repairs and downtime.

- **You'll receive faster support while lowering your repair costs**. Thanks to remote monitoring software, your consultant will be able to access and repair most network problems right over the Internet. No more waiting around for an engineer to show up or paying for travel fees.

- **You'll experience faster performance, fewer problems, and**

practically zero downtime.

- Some components of your network will degrade in performance over time, causing it to slow down, hang up, and crash. The regular preventative maintenance offered through a managed service plan will make sure your computers stay in tip-top shape for maximum speed, performance, and reliability.

- **You'll get top level IT support without the costs and overhead of hiring a full-time IT manager.** A junior technician can easily cost your company $45,000 to $50,000 a year in salary, taxes, and insurance, and a senior consultant could cost two to three times that amount. Under a managed service plan, you get to share a senior consultant with other businesses, to greatly reduce your costs without sacrificing experience or quality of work.

- **You will receive discounts on new projects and better service.** Most computer consultants will offer priority service and a discount to clients on their managed service plan. Plus, your consultant will become more familiar with your hardware, software, settings, and history, and therefore provide much faster service than the consultant who is not familiar and has to spend time "feeling around" your network.

- **You can budget for IT support just like rent or insurance.** If your IT support bill varies from month to month, a managed service plan will help even it out and make budgeting much easier. Just make sure the plan you sign up for is all- inclusive with no hidden charges, caveats, or fees.

- **You will safeguard your data.**

The data on the hard disk is always more important than the hardware that houses it. If you rely on your computer systems for daily operations, it's time to get serious about protecting your critical, irreplaceable electronic information. A good managed service plan will greatly reduce your chances of losing critical company data, files, and information.

- **You'll gain incredible peace of mind.**
  As a business owner, you already have enough to worry about; the last thing you need is a computer crisis. By having a managed service plan in place, it takes that worry off your plate.

What to Look For In a Managed Service Plan

There are a number of factors that will go into what you should look for in a managed service plan. A good consultant will take time to sit down with you and explain your options for support based on your priorities, budget, network complexity, support needed, and conditions of satisfaction. However, here are a few things you'll need to make sure your consultant includes in your agreement.

- **Security patches and updates.**
  Software vendors frequently issue patches to cover known security loopholes in their software. However, not all patches can be easily installed, and some will require specialized knowledge. Not too long ago, Microsoft issued a critical security patch for their XP operating system called Service Pack 2. Although this was a necessary security patch to install, it was not as simple as downloading and installing this patch from Microsoft's website. In some cases, the installation caused system failures and software

conflicts that only a trained professional could fix. When you sign up for a managed service contract, make sure security patches and updates are included in your contract.

- **24-7 Monitoring and Alerts.**
  Your consultant should be able to provide around- the-clock monitoring for your network to look for problems developing under the radar. They should also notify you of problems in advance so that preventative action can be taken.

- **Spam Filtering.**
  Not only is it annoying, but it is the number one way viruses enter a computer network. Ask your consultant to provide a solution to filter spam and monitor for viruses at your gateway.

- **Virus Updates.**
  Unless you've been living under a rock, you know that viruses are a very real and very dangerous threat to your computer network. Since new viruses launch daily, you need to make sure your consultant is monitoring your virus protection 24 hours a day, 7 days a week, and automatically updating your network with new virus definitions as soon as they become available.

Note: Your consultant will often recommend virus software for you to purchase - it is not normally included in a managed service plan.

- **Spyware Scanning and Removal.**
  Like viruses, spyware can cause a number of problems for your network and may even result in identity theft. Symptoms of spyware include excessive pop-up ads, sluggish performance, and strange web browsers opening on your computer that you

did not request. Regulation and protection of spyware should be part of your managed service agreement.

- **System Backup Monitoring.**
Your consultant should monitor your daily system backups to make sure they are working properly, and perform a monthly test restore to make sure your data is available in a usable format. Tape backups are notorious for failing. Even if they appear to be working, the data could be corrupt and useless. We have seen several situations where a company thought their data was secure only to find out that it wasn't once they desperately needed it. As part of a managed service contract, your consultant should monitor and maintain this critical part of your network's security. Some consultants will even offer an off- site data backup solution.

- **Vendor Liaison/Management.**
Quite often, software or hardware will fail due to no fault of your consultants. In that scenario, it's far more convenient to have a consultant that is familiar with your network to deal with the warranty returns and replacements of those parts with the manufacturer rather than to try and deal with it yourself. If you've ever had to call the "customer service" hotline of a technology vendor, you know what a headache it can be. Other vendors include practice management software, Internet providers, web hosting companies, and so on. For convenience, have your consultant agree to be your technology vendor liaison with these companies so you don't have the hassle.

- **Creation of Acceptable User Policies and Training.**
An acceptable user policy is simply the rulebook for what your employees can and can't do with your computer network. An

uneducated employee can accidentally introduce spyware, viruses, hackers, and other major problems into your network. They can also use their work computer and e-mail to access and share unacceptable material (such as pornographic sites or racial content). All it takes is one employee to send an off-color joke to a list of friends from your company's e-mail to start problems for you. In many cases, employees' actions can bring expensive and embarrassing lawsuits against your company. Talk to your consultant about ways to educate and enforce an acceptable user's policy.

- **Adding and Removing New Hardware and Software.**
  You just purchased a new printer and you're anxious to start using it. However, you can't figure out why you keep getting error messages and why you cannot print from Excel. If you had a managed service contract in place that covered hardware and software installation, your consultant would be responsible for making sure it was installed and configured properly, and you wouldn't have to waste one minute dealing with these problems.

- **Adding and Removing Users.**
  Although this seems like a simple thing, user access to your network is a critical security risk that needs to be managed properly to avoid disgruntled employees or unauthorized persons accessing your network. This is especially true if you have remote workers. Make sure this is covered in your managed service contract.

- **Help Desk Support.**
  This would include a mix of phone, remote, and on-site support for you and your employees to answer any number of technical questions and problems. Remember, phone support is not free;

calling your consultant for a "quick" question is a billable event and can cost you anywhere from $25 to $100. Therefore, you want to have some level of remote and on-site support included in your managed service contract.

Keep in mind that this is just a starter list of services to look for. The size and complexity of your network, the security required, and the software and systems you use will largely determine the type of on-going support you need. A good computer consultant will take time to understand your needs and offer multiple plans to choose from. They will also be flexible and allow you to upgrade or downgrade the level of support provided should you discover that your plan is not meeting your needs.

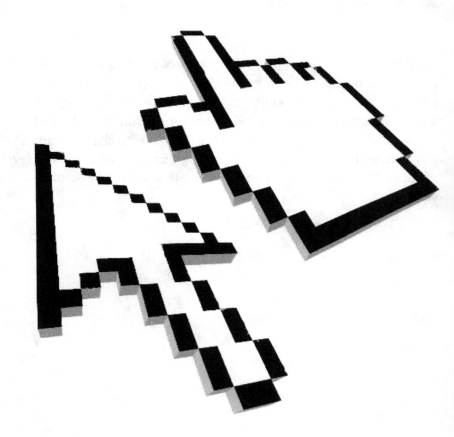

Chapter 7:

Contracts, Payment Schedules, and Rate Negotiations

Now that you've gone through the work of finding the perfect computer consultant, make sure you don't throw all of your hard work down the drain by not securing a clear, concise, win-win contract. A clear and complete contract is your best defense against getting ripped off and disappointed. It also helps both sides completely understand what is expected, how the work will be done, and to what standards. In some instances, it makes sense to have a qualified attorney review your contact. This chapter will outline some of the basic things to include in your contract to make sure you get what you want.

In general, the more detailed the contract is, the better it is for both sides. Don't be afraid of lengthy contracts that spell everything out in specific detail, but DO be cautious of contracts that you don't understand.

Once you've decided on a consultant, ask to meet with them to go over every detail verbally. It is a good idea to prepare for this meeting by outlining your expectations and conditions of satisfaction for the work to be done. The clearer you are on what you want and how you want the work performed, the better your chances are of getting it done right. You should also ask your consultant to bring a copy of his original proposal or quote, as well as a list of deliverables, deadlines, guarantees, and other policies and procedures for how they work.

This meeting is best done in a face-to-face setting. You can negotiate your contract over the phone, but our experience shows that greater clarification and detail comes when we meet face-to-face with our clients.

Warranties, Guarantees, and Making Things Right

One of the main things you want to clarify in your contract is exactly what your consultant does and does not guarantee. Make sure you are as specific as possible. For example, if a computer you purchase through your consultant has a hard drive failure, will your consultant be responsible for getting it replaced with the manufacturer, or will you be? If you experience a problem with the network your consultant recently upgraded or installed, is support included or charged at an extra rate? Also, if you are unhappy with the work, what happens? Will they re-do the job at no extra charge? Will they refund part or all of your money?

Make sure you are very specific on what your consultant will and will not guarantee.

Payment Terms

In most cases, a consultant will require some type of down payment on a project before they will get started, and payment in full for any hardware or software purchases up front. However, you should never pay a consultant in full before a project is started, and you should not be asked to pay the balance of a project until it is completed to your satisfaction. As a rule of thumb, try to reserve as much of the payment as possible until full completion of the project. In some cases, that may be as much as 30-50%. Basically you want to keep the final payment as large as possible to ensure your consultant stays "on the ball" and eager to complete your project.

Regardless of what you agree upon, make sure your agreed upon payment schedule is detailed in a written contract. This would include exact payment dates, amounts, and specifically what work and conditions of satisfaction have to be met before payment is made. Don't be alarmed if your consultant includes a condition that all work will cease for non-payment. This is standard and customary and is not unreasonable.

Project Timeline and Completion Date

If your project is time-sensitive, you'll want to include not only a definite completion date, but also breach of contract terms that give you some type of compensation for every day or week over the agreed upon deadline. Include the phrase that your project is "extremely time-sensitive" and stress the importance of the completion date in writing. That will eliminate any questions or confusions later on regarding the time-sensitive nature of your project.

If your project is lengthy, it makes sense to have a project timeline that includes benchmarks or the phases that your project will be completed in, and payments tied to the completion of these phases. This will keep your consultant on track and prevent you from realizing in the 11th hour that your project is way overdue.

Important: Some projects will require your involvement in testing and approving applications and processes designed by your consultant.

Make sure you allot time in your busy schedule for testing so you don't delay the project.

Changes, Modifications, and "Scope Creep"

Scope creep is a common term used by consultants to describe the changes and modifications clients request to a project after the contract has been signed. In some cases, these "tiny" changes result in more work for the consultant and delays in the project's timeline.

For example, let's suppose you decide it's time to upgrade your network. Your consultant provides you a game plan and a quote for what it will take to upgrade your entire system.
However, halfway through the project you decide that you want to give your traveling sales team secure remote access to the network - something that was not discussed in the original project and proposal. Although it seems to be a simple request, it may take additional hardware, software, and hours of work to set up a secure remote connection.

Therefore, it's normal and customary for a consultant to outline an hourly rate for any and all projects, changes, and tasks requested by you, the client, *after* the contract has been signed. Just make sure that the hourly rate or amount for any changes is not unreasonable, *and* that it is clearly defined in the contract you sign. In most cases, the consultant will agree to a discounted rate for additional work resulting from changes you make to the original agreement. Again, be sure you have that rate in writing so they don't double their rates halfway into your project.

A word of caution! Whenever you request a change to your existing contract or scope of work, make sure you get the change order in writing.

If your consultant is a professional, they will require you to sign a written contract addendum. If they don't, make sure you press for one. Do not fall into the trap of verbal "he said - she said" agreements; they will only come back to haunt you later. All change orders should include:

- The specific changes to be made
- The date of the request
- A detailed description of the work to be done
- Your conditions of satisfaction
- The additional charges
- Guarantees or warranties
- A new completion date for your project (if necessary)

This document should be signed by both you and your consultant.

Hardware, Software, and Materials

Many computer consultants will gladly research and quote the cost of various hardware and software for the completion of a project. Some will even offer to custom build your server and workstations instead of purchasing them from a hardware distributor. In most cases, these non-branded computers are every bit as reliable as branded machines offered by Dell, HP, or Compaq. Either way, you want to keep in mind that your consultant is probably not making a lot of money on selling you hardware and software, and in many cases, will only resell it to you as a convenience for you (one stop shop).

That is why you want to detail in your contract who is responsible for the warranty on the equipment. If something goes wrong, do you want your consultant to handle it, or will you? Most consultants will charge for handling the warranty repairs on your equipment. Do not make the mistake of assuming that because they sold it to you, they are then responsible for manufacturer defects, or that they will do the repairs for free. If you expect them to handle this, then you must detail that in your contract.

Hours and Conditions of Work

Another point you want to consider before signing on the dotted line is how and when the work will be completed. One of the biggest inconveniences of having a consultant work on your network is the downtime it costs you.

In some situations, it may be necessary for you and all of your employees to log off the network so your consultant may complete certain tasks. If you only need to log off for a short period of time, this is only a minor inconvenience. However, if you are upgrading your entire network, or if you are installing a new system, you could be down for several hours.

To prevent your business from being disrupted for long periods of time, ask your consultant how much downtime the repair or project will require. If you cannot afford to be offline for that long, ask that any major upgrades, installations, or repairs be done after hours or on weekends. It may cost a bit more, but most consultants will gladly accommodate you if you ask in advance.

Arbitration and Cancellation Clauses

While this book is dedicated to helping you find a great consultant that you will never want to fire, there still is a chance that you could end up hiring the wrong guy. If that happens, you want to make sure your contract is written to protect your rights and prevent you from being taken advantage of. Again, this section should not be considered legal advice and it should not take the place of a qualified attorney reviewing your contact; however, for the sake of completeness, we will touch on what you need to look for to protect yourself in the event that your consultant doesn't fulfill on his promises.

First, make sure you include an arbitration clause in your contract. Arbitration is often a faster, easier, and less expensive way to resolve a dispute between you and the consultant you hired. Some consultants will specify an arbitration company in their contract. If you don't like their choice, make sure you voice your concern and recommend an alternative independent arbitration company. Again, make sure it's in writing.

Next, make sure your contract has a clear cancellation policy. If you discover that you hired the wrong guy and want out of your contract, you'll want a written clause that details not only how to cancel the contract, but also what you will owe. Determining whether or not you are entitled to a refund or required to pay for work completed will often have to be negotiated by the arbitration company you designate in your contract.

Quick Tip: If you decide you need to cancel a contract, make sure you send your cancellation notice by certified mail, return receipt requested. This will give you proof that your consultant has received your cancellation notice.

The biggest "secret" to securing a win-win contract is to make sure there are no loopholes. Include everything you can think of in writing, no matter how small or insignificant it may seem at the moment.

And finally, you should always have a qualified legal consultant review your agreement, especially if it involves a lengthy and expensive project. The little bit of money you will invest in a good attorney will go a long way to ensure a happy, hassle-free project!

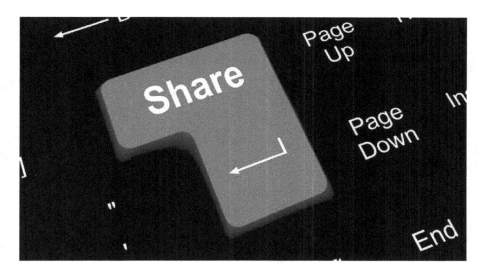

Chapter 8:

Technical Terms Explained in Plain English

ADSL: Short for *Asymmetrical Digital Subscriber Line*, a high-speed Internet service delivered over a telephone line where the transmit and receive speeds are unequal.
Typically, the download speed (the speed at which the user receives information) is significantly higher than the upload speed. Typically, this service is better for home users and is not ideal for business use.

ASP: Short for *Application Service Provider*, a third-party company that manages and distributes software-based services and solutions to their customers over a wide area network, usually the Internet.

Content Filtering: Software that prevents users from accessing or sending objectionable content via your network. Although this usually refers to web content, many programs also screen inbound and outbound e-mails for offensive and confidential information. This software is not designed for virus, worm, or hacker prevention.

CPU: Abbreviation for *Central Processing Unit*, the brains of a computer.

DHCP: Short for *Dynamic Host Configuration Protocol*, a method for dynamically assigning IP addresses to devices upon request, rather than explicitly programming an IP address into each device. If you have a server on your network, configuring that server as a DHCP server will make it much easier to add or reconfigure individual workstations on the network.

Default Gateway: In a TCP/IP Network, this is the gateway in a network that computers on that network use to send and receive data to other computers and networks outside of the local network. Typically this is the router or firewall that connects the local network to the public Internet, although it might also be a router that connects to another remote server or computer within the same company.

DMZ: Short for *Demilitarized Zone*, a separate area of your network that is isolated from both the Internet and your protected internal network. A DMZ is usually created by your firewall to provide a location for devices such as Web servers that you want to be accessible from the public Internet.

DNS: Short for *Domain Name System (or Server)*, an Internet service that translates domain names into IP addresses. Even though most domain names are alphabetic, hardware devices (like your PC) can only send data to a specific IP address. When you type www.microsoft.com into your web browser, or send an e-mail message to someone@business.com, your Web browser and e-mail server have to be able to look up the IP address that corresponds to the Microsoft.com web server, or to the mail server that receives e-mail for business.com. DNS is the mechanism for doing this lookup.

DSL: Short for *Digital Subscriber Line*, a high-speed Internet service delivered over a telephone line.

Firewall: A device or software program designed to protect your network from unauthorized access over the Internet. It may also provide NAT (Network Address Translation) and VPN (Virtual Private Network) functionality.

FT1: See "T1"

IP Address: An identifier for a computer or device on a TCP/IP network. The format for an IP address is a 32-bit numeric address separated by periods (example: 207.46.20.60).
Within an isolated network you can assign an IP address at random, as long as each IP address on that network is unique. However, if you are connecting a network or computer to the Internet, you must have a registered IP address (also called an Internet address) to avoid duplicates.

ISP: Short for *Internet Service Provider*, the company that provides you with access to the Internet.

POP3: Short for *Post Office Protocol 3,* a method of communication between an e-mail server and an e-mail client. In most cases, when the client software connects to a POP3 server, the e-mail messages are downloaded to the client and are no longer available on the server.

Protocol: An agreed-upon format for transmitting data between two devices.

SDSL: Short for *Symmetrical Digital Subscriber Line*, a high-speed Internet service delivered over a telephone line where the transmit and receive speeds are equal. SDSL service is usually more expensive than ADSL service, but is generally more stable and more suitable for business applications, especially if the business intends to utilize Voice- Over-IP (VoIP).

T1: A dedicated digital transmission line that sends and receives data at a rate of 1.544 Mbps. T1 lines can be used to carry voice traffic, data traffic, or a combination of both.

TCP/IP: Short for *Transmission Control Protocol/Internet Protocol*, the basic language that governs traffic on the entire global Internet, as well as on most private networks.

URL: Short for *Uniform Resource Locator,* the global address of documents, website, and other resources on the World Wide Web.

VoIP: Short for Voice-Over-IP, a category of hardware and software that allows you to use the Internet to make phone calls and send faxes. This technology is becoming very popular with businesses and home users alike because it greatly reduces telephone costs.

VPN: Short for *Virtual Private Network* which is a network constructed by using public wires (the Internet) to connect nodes (usually computers and servers). A VPN uses encryption and other security mechanisms to ensure that only authorized users can access the network and the data it holds. This allows businesses to connect to other servers and computers located in remote offices, from home, or while traveling.

An Invitation to the Reader

The reason I published this book was to educate business owners with the basic knowledge they need to make a great decision when choosing a computer consultant. I believe that a great computer consultant can contribute to your businesses success just like a great marketing consultant, attorney, accountant, or financial advisor.

The technology industry is so new, and growing at such a rapid pace, that most business owners can't keep up with all of the latest whiz-bang gadgets, alphabet soup acronyms, and choices available to them. Plus, many of the "latest and greatest" technological developments have a shelf life of six months before they become obsolete or completely out of date. Sorting through this rapidly moving mess of information to formulate an intelligent plan for growing a business requires a true professional who not only understands technology and how it works, but also understands how people and businesses need to work with technology for true progress.

Unfortunately, the complexity of technology makes it easy for a business owner to fall victim to an incompetent or dishonest computer consultant. When this happens, it creates feelings of mistrust towards all technology consultants and vendors, which makes it difficult for those of us striving to deliver exceptional value and service to our clients.

Therefore, my purpose is to not only arm the small business owner with the information they need to find an honest, competent computer consultant, but in doing so, to raise the standards and quality of services for all consultants in my industry. I believe that the more this topic is discussed, the better it will become for all involved.

I certainly want your feedback on the ideas contained within this book. If you've tried the strategies I've outlined and they worked, please send me your story. If you've had a bad experience with a computer consultant, we want to hear those horror stories as well. If you have additional tips and insights that we have not considered, please share them with me. We might even use them in a future book!

Again, the more aware you are of what it takes to find and hire great consultants in every aspect of your business - not just technology - the stronger your business will become. I am truly passionate about building an organization that delivers uncommon service to my customers. I want to help business owners see the true competitive advantages technology can deliver to their business, and not just view it as an expensive necessity and source of problems.

Your contributions, thoughts, and stories pertaining to this will make this possible. Please write, call, or e-mail me with your ideas.

Our (Swift Chip's) Client Bill of Rights:

1. You should not have to chase your computer consultant. When you have a problem, we feel that you should be able to get help fast. That is why we guarantee your phone call will either be answered immediately when you call or returned within 60 minutes or less by an experienced technician who can help.

2. You should not have to wait around all day for your computer consultant to show up. That is why we offer remote support to all our clients. This service allows us to access your network remotely and drastically reduce the amount of time it takes to resolve your problem. If we cannot resolve your issue remotely, we will immediately dispatch a technician to your office.

3. You deserve to get answers to your questions in PLAIN ENGLISH. Our technicians will not talk down to you or make you feel stupid because you don't understand their "geek speak".

4. You deserve complete satisfaction with all of our work. We will not make excuses or dismiss your requests. Our team is committed to doing whatever it takes to make you happy and complete every job to your expectations. No hassles, no problems.

5. You should EXPECT that no damage will be done to your network or your data.
Before we start working on your computer or network, we will evaluate your problem and alert you to any potential risks involved in fulfilling your job. If there are any risks, they will be explained in full, and your authorization and agreement will be obtained before the

work commences. You can also choose to have your data backed up before we start any work on your machine.

A large proportion of our business comes from referrals from happy, satisfied customers. We want you to recommend us and we know that you will only do this if you are happy with the services we provide. That is why we work so hard to go above and beyond the call of duty.

FREE 27-Point

Problem Prevention Audit
($138 Value)

Don't let computer problems take over your business! If you are a business owner with 5 or more PCs, I'd like to offer you a FREE 27- Point Problem Prevention Network Audit to:

- Diagnose any on-going problems or concerns you have with the computers on your network.

- Scan for hidden viruses, spyware, and loopholes in your network security that could allow hackers and other cyber-criminals to access your confidential information.

- Check your system backups to make sure they are not corrupted and can be recovered in case of an emergency.

- Review your network configuration and peripheral devices to make sure you are getting the maximum performance and speed from your machines.

- Review your server file logs to look for looming problems or conflicts that can cause unexpected downtime.

- Check that all security updates and patches are in place.

Call us today and mention code "Book1" to learn more or to schedule your FREE Computer Network Audit

Swift Chip, Inc.
433 N. Camden Dr., 6th Fl.
Beverly Hills, CA 90210

1-866-326-2008

http://swiftchipinc.com

About the author:

Kenneth May is the co-owner of Swift Chip, Inc., a full service IT company with locations in Beverly Hills, and Ventura, California. They service all of Los Angeles, Ventura, and Southern Santa Barbara Counties.

He has a bachelor's degree in Liberal Arts Degree from Thomas Aquinas College, a Master's degree from the Santa Barbara COM, and has studied in Japan and China.

He hosts a radio show called "*Tech Today with Ken May*" on AM1400 KKZZ, and is streamable at his blog at http://kenmay.net, and iTunes.

He is happily married and has two beautiful little girls.

Mr. May's passions include travel, music and Chinese Martial Arts.